The Art of War: A Memoir of Life in Prison with Mafia, Serial Killers and Sex Offenders Who Get Stabbed (Life in Lockdown # 3)

Published by Glenn Langohr @
http://www.audiobookprisonstories.com

Copyright 2013 by Glenn Langohr, Amazon Edition
All rights reserved. No part of this publication may be reproduced, transmitted, copied or scanned in any form or by any means, without prior written permission by the copyright holder.

This book is based on true events in the author's life. Some timelines, events, places and names have been changed for dramatic purposes

Chapter 1

Business as usual

I stood at the cell door staring. My adrenaline was still pumping. I had just slammed an ice pick into an inmate's neck that was in prison for beating his wife to a pulp in front of his daughter. One of the prison guards had exposed the grisly details.

After I had stabbed him in the neck, my cell brother had thrown the ice pick over one of the buildings. It was sitting in the dirt on the other side of the fence, barely visible.

Godwin, the wife beater who terrorized his daughter, leaked blood in tiny rivers down his body and walked around in a daze until one of the prison guards noticed and hit the alarm.

One of the guards called it in through his microphone and the main gun tower responded by yelling through a microphone, "EVERYONE GET DOWN! DOWN ON THE GROUND FLAT! DON'T MOVE UNTIL WE TELL YOU!"

That's all it took. Over 100 White and Asian inmates immediately got on the ground while the building guards ran out of five different buildings.

Everyone watched a couple of guards sit Godwin on the ground. Then the medics came running. Then the gate to D Yard opened and another team of medics ran to Godwin with a stretcher. After a few minutes of studying his neck wound, they hoisted him onto the gurney and pushed him off the yard.

We stayed on the ground watching for another twenty minutes before the Inmate Gang Investigators, known as I.G.I, or Goon Squad, arrived with crime scene tape and cameras.

They found some blood on the asphalt and took pictures but never set up the crime scene tape. Probably because it wasn't a serious enough injury or they hadn't found a weapon.

Next, the Goon Squad stripped every inmate naked for a brief search and took a statement in patches all over the yard.

He got to us. After taking off my clothes and squatting and coughing I got dressed again and answered, "I was right here. I didn't see nothin."

Damon had followed suit.

The prison guards and Goon Squad had coordinated it so that inmates from one building at a time were escorted back to their building.

I shook off the memory from a couple hours ago and stared out the cell at the wall underneath the gun tower. In red block letters it stated: WARNING: NO WARNING SHOTS FIRED, WARDEN

Damon was on the top bunk behind me and asked, "How long do you think we'll be on lockdown for that?"

I looked at the gun tower. It was bullet proof Plexiglas that was tinted grey but you could see two regular guards watching the yard. They were probably watching the other guards search for the weapon.

I said, "Probably not more than a day or two. That wasn't very serious. No more than a bee sting. He's lucky we didn't make a handle for that ice pick."

With a handle, the ice pick would have slammed deeper into his neck.

Damon said, "You're heart wasn't in it was it?"

I shook my head that it wasn't.

We had bigger problems to worry about. Nine months ago our race, the White inmates were beaten unconscious in a yard riot outnumbered in a bad way by the Mexicans over an out of control drug debt. Seventeen White inmates were rushed off the yard on stretchers. Some needed facial reconstruction. Some had boot prints embedded in their faces.

The White inmates only made up 8% of the prison population here.

Another problem, one of the prison guards, a Security Escort by the name of Heart, was feeding us information and helping us with a few things. It was good and bad. He told us we had a notorious child molester who had 44 counts of penetration on God knew how many kids. We were waiting for him to furnish us the proof in the form of court paperwork.

Chapter 2

Enter Mark Grisham

The 400 pound steel vestibule door shrieked and clanged open for five seconds. The two guards in the tower watched someone walk underneath, then through the twenty-foot long tunnel into the building.

I said, "It's Mark Grisham already!"

Mark was a 51-year-old White inmate with a northern Italian heritage. He was wise as a fox and looked like one with a ton of smile lines on a big expressive face and baldhead. He had just as many mental issues as us and covered them up in a similar way to me, by grinding his lips together in an ADHD trait, concentration mode.

He worked in the program office where all the guards checked in and some stayed to work. There were Administrators, Lieutenants and Sergeants. He took care of their dirty work, the typing of almost all the documents; the rest was a cat and mouse game of which side could extract information and favors. Mark was pretty good, but he worried us with his "social butterfly, overly talkative style" We kept him in check with a healthy dose of stress to keep him focused and on his toes. If we pushed to hard, his happy go lucky infectious smiles and demeanor were gone. We realized his "happy, care free" demeanor was a good face for calm when dealing with other inmate races, like the Mexican Mobsters in the cell next to us, the Black Gangster Crip and Blood gangs and the Vietnamese killers. He was the temperature gage and face of our race.

He climbed the stairs wearing state issue blue denim jeans that posted yellow block letters on the left hip: CDC, for California Department of Corrections. He was wearing a similar blue button down collared shirt that had creases that could draw blood. He turned the corner on the way to our cell and from the half-inch crack on the side I studied his eyes underneath clear, square reading glasses.

His blue eyes were focused on something internal in concentration mode and his lips were clamped together.

Having just come from the Program Office, he had information about the stabbing.

I asked, "How long we going to be locked down?"

He said, "I don't know yet."

Mark's face was filling the 4-inch wide Plexiglas at our cell door and a tiny smile broke through his gritted teeth.

Mark came over to the side of our cell to talk quiet enough so only we could hear. He said, "You guys don't waste any time."

It was our second day on the mainline.

Mark said, "Heart is impressed. He asked me who you had do it?"

The vestibule clanked and grinded open. One of the guards in the tower walked from the yard window with whoever was walking in the tunnel underneath.

Security Escort Heart walked into the building with his partner Ligazzaro behind him. They walked into the building for 20 feet to greet our building guard Garcia.

Next to me, Damon grunted, "Heart is crazy if he thinks you're going to tell him who stabbed Godwin."

I said, "Tell Heart that he stabbed him. He's the one who sealed Godwin's fate by telling us his criminal history."

Security Escort Heart had escorted Damon and I from the bus to D Yard almost a month ago where we stayed locked down until a couple days ago. He told us about the inmate race riots on the yard and the rest of the prison politics we needed to be aware of. On one hand, the information was vital to our survival strategies, but on the other hand, he was overly involved and pushing to hard.

Mark asked point blank, "Did you guys stab Godwin?"

My lips grinded together in frustration and I said, "We don't need a bunch of publicity."

Damon said, "That wasn't a stabbing. That was just physical therapy."

Heart looked at our cell from the podium and walked to the stairs. He walked to our cell and Damon muttered, "The nerve of this guy. We might as well hang a sign above our cell that says, Shot Callers."

Our Mexican Mobster neighbors made their presence felt by tapping on their cell door. I heard Boxer say, "Mark!"

Before Mark moved us next to the Mobsters for diplomatic relations, with Heart's help, he might as well have been Mexican or a coat rack, because he had been hanging at the side of their cell every time he was in the building and not locked in his cell. Boxer and Sano had dominated his time and picked his brain as if he were in their cell with them.

Boxer had spent the last five years seven floors under ground, in the highest security prison in the nation in Colorado. Sano was another Mexican Mobster pretty high up the chain.

We moved next to them as leaders for the White inmates so we could develop relations for peace for both races.

It was our second day next to the Mobsters and the second time Mark was at our cell looking at us to see if we were done talking. He was halfway to their cell like a magnet was pulling on him from both directions.

Heart was a few feet from our cell and I looked away from Mark's stretched out stressed face in dismissal to see what Heart was doing.

Heart stopped at our cell and my attention was just as divided as Marks.

I heard Boxer say quietly, "They got away with it huh?"

Damon and I had told Boxer and Sano that we were handling the business personally. It was a trust thing. We knew Mexican Mobsters didn't incriminate anyone.

We heard Mark say, "I didn't see them do it and they aren't telling me who did."

Heart had some court paperwork in his hands and he positioned it at the side of our cell door where the small crack was and slid it in.

I didn't grab it and stopped Damon's hand as he tried to reach for it. The paperwork was about an inmate who had 44 counts of Child Molestation. It might as well have been a bomb. It was going to force us to slice part of his face off. I didn't like the position we were in. I didn't want to force some kid to handle it, who wouldn't know how, and I didn't want to force a seasoned convict to do it who could catch a 3rd strike and life sentence over it.

I waved Heart to the side of the cell door.

He positioned his back against the wall so his ear was inches from my lips at the side of the cell, just like a convict. I asked, "Are you going to help us get away with this one?"

Heart turned to talk into my ear through the side of the cell. "You didn't need my help today did you?"

Damon laughed and it forced me to relax. I grabbed the paperwork.

Truthfully, I was in over my head. I wanted enough control of the White inmates to keep us all safe, with level headed policies, like drug debt rules and other regulations to keep us tight, but this level of familiarity with a prison guard was new to me. Was I supposed to ask for dope, a cell phone or tobacco?

I responded, "Yeah but this one is more serious. Someone could catch a life case over this child predator."

Heart said, "Just don't kill him and the investigation won't be serious. We let you guys get away with a lot on the yard."

Heart tapped on our cell door and went next door.

We watched him get in line next to Mark.

We barely heard Mark say, "It was nice to meet you Sano. The I.G.I. is going to take you to the hole any time. Pack your stuff."

We heard Sano laugh and say, "My stuff is always packed."

Mark noticed Heart standing there and got out of the way. I waved him back over to our cell.

Damon asked Mark, "Are they taking both of em?"

Mark stayed in front of our cell and shook his head. He was looking next door and trying to listen to what they were saying.

Heart was whispering into the side of their cell with his back to the wall. I looked at Garcia sitting at the podium below. He was watching. He said something into his microphone on his shoulder to the guard in the tower.

The guard in the tower tapped the microphone to signify an announcement. "Attention on the tier. The yard is on lockdown pending an investigation. Mark Grisham lock it up!"

Mark came to the side of our cell and said, "They're taking Sano and leaving Boxer for right now. They don't have enough room for both of them in the hole."

Mark knocked on the door goodbye and walked to his cell six doors away.

A couple minutes later Heart said good-bye to Boxer and Sano and walked past our cell. I pounded on the door and yelled, "Heart! How long are the White inmates going to be locked down?"

Heart stopped walking for just long enough to say, "Anywhere from a couple days to two weeks. They'll have a meeting about it tomorrow."

Chapter 3

Boxer's Calling Shots Solo for the Chicanos

We heard our Mexican Mobster neighbors' pound on the wall. I got off my bunk and got on the ground on all fours and banged on the wall back.

Boxer said, "I'm sending my line!"

I said, "Shoot it!"

Before we went to yard and gave Godwin a "soft whacking", we had sent our homemade wine to their cell to keep it safe.

A line came flying into our cell carried by a milk carton container that had been smashed flat and weighted down with just enough state soap. I pulled the line in and felt it resist and heard the sound of liquid sloshing around. Our vino.

I heard Boxer say, "There's a "wila" in there "tambien." *Mexican prison slang for a written message also.*

I pulled the message out of a slot in the milk carton and handed it to my cell brother Damon.

Damon read it to me while I pulled in our not quite ready alcohol.

"Greetings BJ and Damon, glad you made it back from your mission. As you probably know, Sano is going back to the hole. Do you want to send any messages to your people in there? With Respect, Boxer and Sano"

They were following protocol. Our races were allied together. We shared the same spaces on the yard, we shared the same showers in the building and we even worked out together as if we were in the military and on the same side, at certain influential prisons. We passed messages for each other, fed each other and in general, cared for and respected each other.

Right now, they were asking if we wanted to send a message to anyone in the hole Solitary Confinement.

If we would have known who the "Shot Caller" for the White inmates was in the hole, it would have made us appear very organized and given us even more clout.

It always helped to have a Mexican Mobster on the yard because business was done right and riots didn't happen, unless they had to. Right now, one was on going between the Mexican and the Black inmates. Mexican pride was on the line after receiving a beat down six months prior.

We heard our neighbor's bang on our wall again. Boxer asked, "Do you guys want to read the newspaper? We got the Orange County Register over here!"

I got down on the ground again and yelled, "Yeah, shoot it please!"

I got our line out and pinched it with my thumb as close as possible to the corner of our cell and extended the line with the milk carton far enough to wing it in a circular motion. By holding it pinched to the ground it flew out and under the cell door in an arc that brought it right under their cell door. We heard it whack their wall and I felt it get pulled in further.

A couple minutes later I pulled in the line with the newspaper wrapped around it.

Damon was on the top bunk studying the paperwork Heart gave us.

I gave him some space to get a brain full of stress and tried to act nonchalant by reading our hometown news.

As fate would have it, on the front page of the Orange County Register, there was an article about a friend of mine. His name was Jared Petrovich. He was a youngster at 22 years old.

I knew him when he was a 16-year-old runaway drug addict. He was absolutely harmless. Or he was then.

Now he was fighting a life sentence!

The article stated that he had been to prison for a sentence of a year, since I'd last seen him. Now, fighting another drug addict case for petty theft, he was being charged with a high profile murder beef in our county jail. The authorities were even saying he was a "Shot Caller", who organized the "Hit".

But there was way more to the ugly story.

An Orange County Jail Deputy had told some of the Mexican and White inmates that they had a high profile "Child Molester" in their domain, his name, John Chamberlain.

The article alluded to the possibility that a few Sheriff deputies helped the inmates "handle the business" by leaving their watch post for a while.

They were housed in a dormitory setting that was considered "low level" in the F Barracks at Theo Lacy Branch Jail.

I knew that part of the county jail. The Deputies had to have helped them by leaving their post. It was impossible for them not to see and hear the attack otherwise.

I read between the lines and visualized what happened. The Sheriff deputy probably "alerted" way to many inmates about the "Child Molester" living with them, way to loudly, and that presented an enormous amount of stress.

The reason I deduced that it happened that way is because the article went on to state that three Mexican inmates and three White inmates were involved in the beat down that ended in Chamberlain's death.

The mission had been put together haphazardly.

The Deputies turned a blind eye for to long. By the time they came back to their posts, medical attention was a tad to late.

Even worse, Chamberlain wasn't even a Child Molester.

He was in jail for "Possessing Child Pornography".

If the inmates had been more seasoned, they would have forced the Sheriff to turn over the court "Paperwork" to reinforce the claim before acting.

Damon broke through my reading by asking, "What does this penal code reference mean? ANNLY/MOLEST…"

I handed Damon the article to read and accepted the paperwork for Daniel Dennings.

There were 6 legal papers stapled together. The first two pages stated that Daniel Dennings had been charged with 72 charges. There were 44 counts of ANNLY/MOLEST that started on Jan 1, 1994. For the purposes of sentencing Daniel Dennings was found guilty on Jan 15, 1994, then on Feb 1, 1994, then on Feb 15, 1994 and so on for the entire 44 counts. Then his lesser charges were listed that included: Sodomy, oral copulation and lewd and lascivious behavior.

What the heck did ANNLY/MOLEST stand for? My mind flashed images of the worst Catholic priest scenario forcing anal and oral sex on a little boy, or a bunch of them.

My Friend Jared Petrovich who told Orange County Reporters, "The cops who told me John Chamberlain was a Child Molester are just as guilty."

Chapter 4

So Cal Politics

The Mexican and Black inmates had been locked down 24 hours a day 7 days a week for the last 6 months, except for medical visits, and showers 3 times a week, separately.

Now that Sano was waiting for an escort to the hole, there was a vacuum of power to be replaced. It was time to watch the reaction.

On the way out the building Heart stopped to tell Garcia something, and Garcia sent word to the guard in the gun tower.

They watched their cell. They weren't the only ones watching.

The Black inmates felt the winds of change on the horizon. A few in cells nearby probably heard the news like we did. Throughout the building, the Black inmates filled 37 of the 100 cells, and each cell had two bodies crammed in front watching.

This prison in Imperial Valley on the California side of the Mexican border, housed some veteran Black inmates. It didn't look like any of them had done less then 10 years of hard core prison time and most looked like they had done closer to 20. It showed by how gigantic they were from working out. It showed even more by how quiet and respectful they were.

We had been studying them during the every other day showers.

We heard the gun tower guard tap on the microphone to signify an announcement and every one watched him lean forward. "Attention in the building! We are running showers for the Black inmates!"

Every cell in the building had two inmates standing at the door watching. During inmate race wars and gang wars there was always the chance of violence. There was a possibility that the wrong cell doors would get opened, unintentionally, or intentionally.

If the gun tower guard at the control booth was evil, or just complacent, he could open a Black cell and a Mexican cell at the same time and there would surely be a mini war.

Inmates doing life sentences, gang members who swore allegiance to their neighborhood pride and mentally distraught humans who couldn't take any more stress were known to come out of the cell with weapons on a suicide mission.

The sounds of cell doors popping open in the deathly quiet building started.

"Pop!" "Pop!" "Pop!"

Below us and across the building, cell 103 had two giant Black men gangsta stroll their way down the tier toward their shower with towels wrapped around necks.

They stopped at the next cell that opened at 107 where two more Black men stayed inside getting ready. A tall and skinny snoop dog looking Crip gang member inched his way out of the cell and half hugged each of the other inmates while his cell brother grabbed a couple of books to give or trade away.

Fifteen minutes later the next group of Black men showered and the tension in the building died down. It didn't look like any mistakes were going to be made, unintentionally, or intentionally.

Standing next to me, Damon said what I was already thinking, "Garcia won't let nothing scandalous go down in his building…"

Garcia was watching everything like a hawk from the middle of the building from his podium. He was a veteran prison guard who was very clear in how he ran things. We were allowed to communicate, drink alcohol, and smoke tobacco and tattoo on each other as long as we didn't "front him off" and as long as we kept the violence on the yard.

We heard Mark yell out of his cell, "Garcia! Can I get my shower when you get a chance?"

Garcia nodded and said something into the microphone on his shoulder and the gun tower guard immediately popped his cell.

Mark came to our cell. I felt so much stress over Daniel Denning's Child Molestation paper work that I had to force some stress on him.

I put my finger to my lips for him to see to be quiet and waved him to the side of the cell.

I whispered urgently into his ear. "Check this out homeboy, not a peep of this pedophile noise can get out. If it does it's your fault and you'll have to clean it up."

I stepped away from the crack at the side of the cell and waited for Mark to understand that I was waiting for him to look at us through the Plexiglas.

Almost a minute passed and he got in front of our cell to see Damon's dead serious expression reinforcing how vital our situation was.

I waved him back and whispered why we were extremely stressed. "If this baby rapist finds out his number is up by people not talking to him, or his cell brother acting different, our life is in danger for not handling it."

I stepped away from his ear and thought about the problem. If Daniel Denning's caught on and told a prison guard he was in fear for his life, the prison administration would follow protocol and send him to one of the other 3 yards. That would send the problem over there. The White inmates would possibly find out the same bad news and would realize we had blown it.

By having him sliced or stabbed, to get him sent to another prison, inmates could catch life sentences. Southern California prison justice is absolute. Our lack of leadership would have to be regulated. We could be stabbed over it.

Mark again looked at how serious we were and I waved the Orange County Register at him and said loud enough to speak through the middle of the cell door, "There's a front page story you should read."

I dropped the paper on the ground and pushed it with my foot under the cell.

Mark grabbed it and came to the side of the cell and whispered, "Stop stressing homeboys. This isn't my first rodeo. My lips are sealed."

I felt my face loosen up and I smiled through gritted teeth.

Damon pushed me out of the way to make room for his lips to whisper a second round of questioning. "What cell is this child torturer in?"

Mark whispered, "He's in Building 3 on the bottom tier in cell 126."

Damon asked the next most important question, "Who's in the cell with him?"

That was where the problem should have been handled. It made whoever was inside look almost as bad for not running a tight enough program to know. Did he know and essentially condone it? Was he hiding something also?"

Mark whispered, "Some ancient dude doing a life sentence. I think he's in his late 60's. His name is Richard."

Damon whispered what I was wondering, "Is he any good? Has anyone checked his paperwork?"

In California prisons, the Administration usually housed like kind people together. Once Daniel Dennings was stabbed or sliced, he'd go to a protective custody yard where other Child Molesters were. It was possible that Richard was doing his time for something similar.

Mark whispered, "Heart said Richard is doing life for murdering his wife."

Damon whispered, "That figures. He's a curb creature predator too."

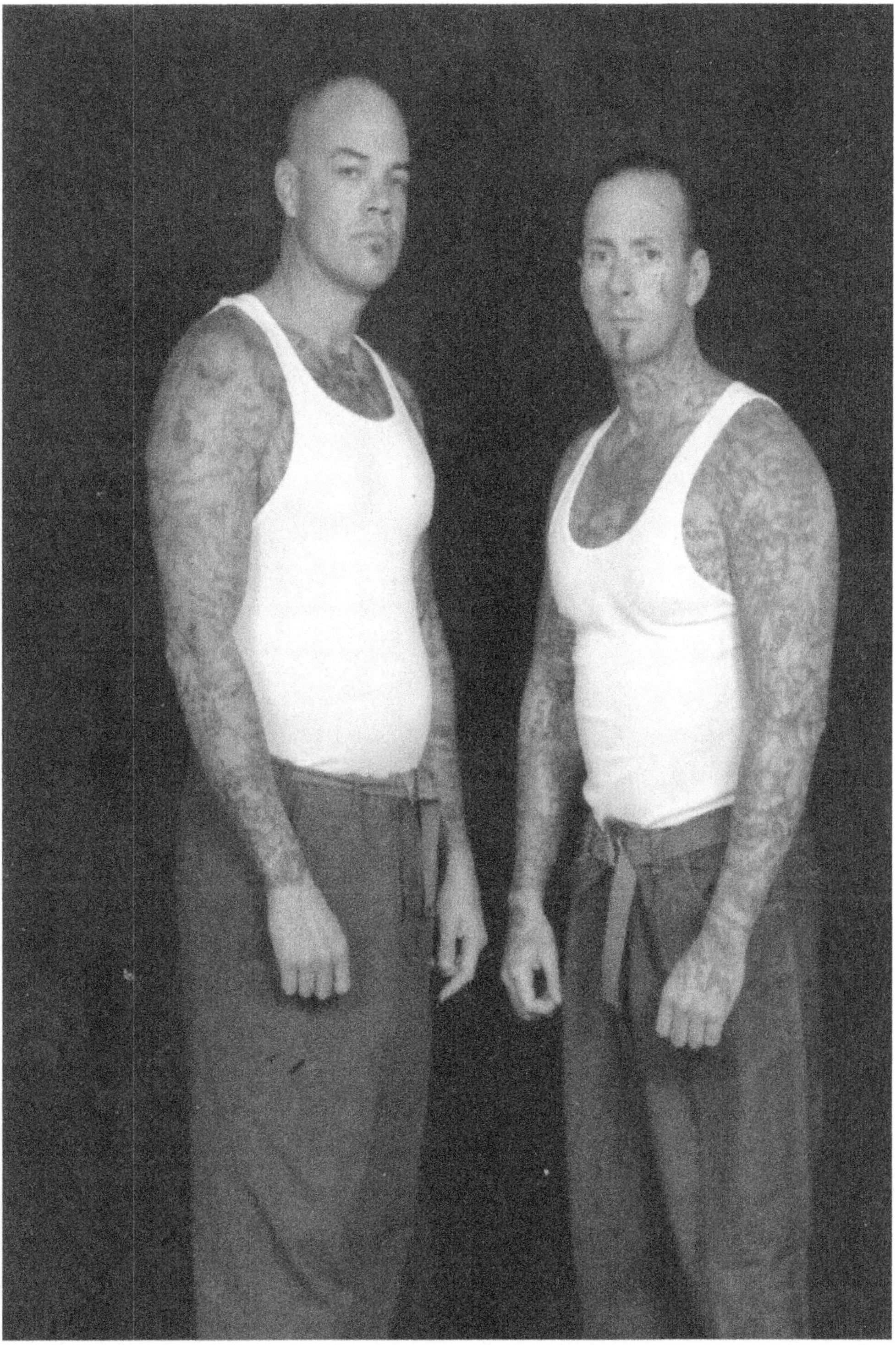

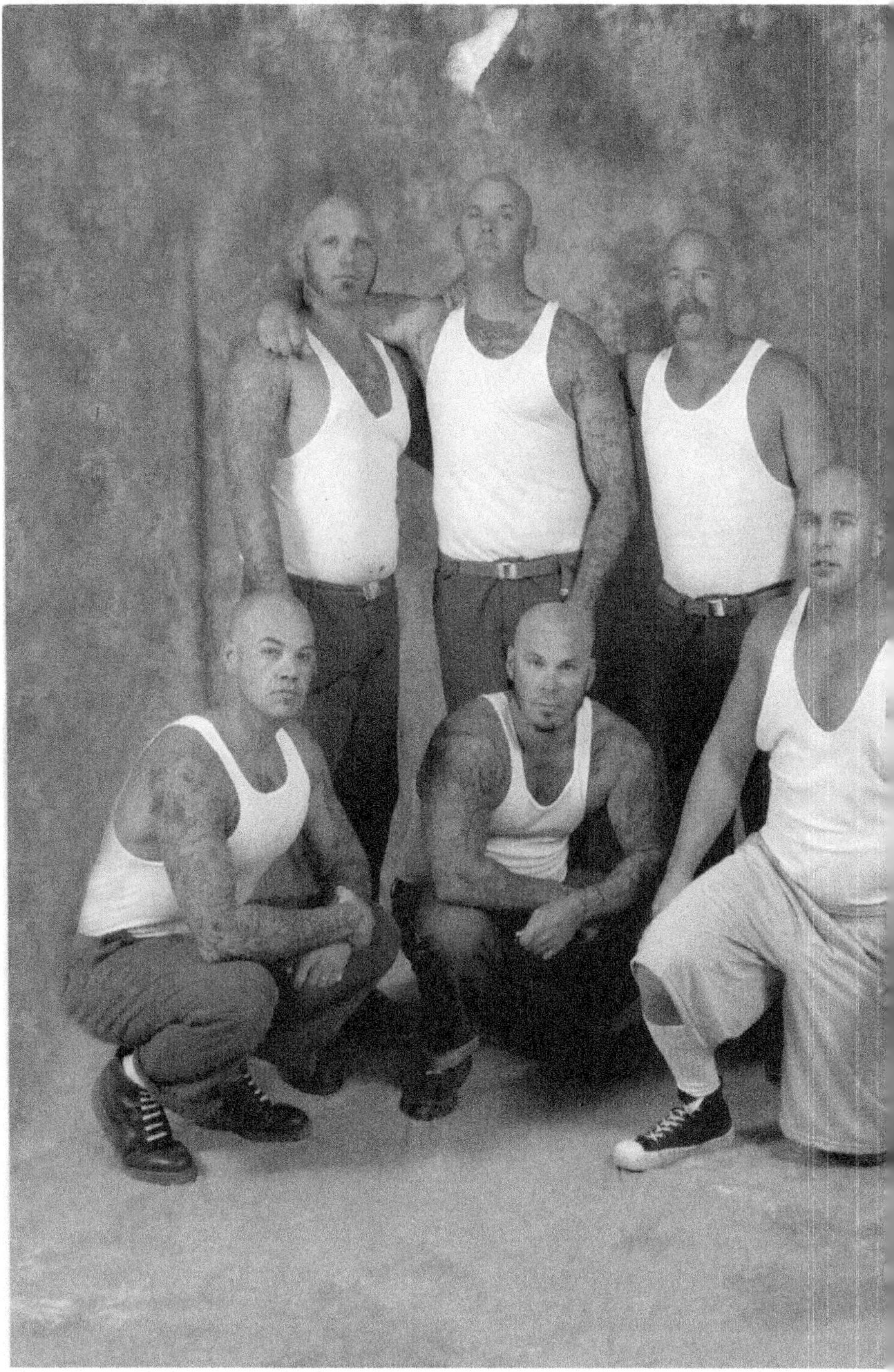

Chapter 5

A Middle of the Night Raid

At 3 a.m. a squadron of 13 I.G.I. Gooners entered our building. They came in like paratroopers through a rarely used side door to avoid the loud screeching of the vestibule that would have alerted everyone.

I woke up to our neighbor's cell door popping open and got up already knowing what I'd see.

The I.G.I. Gooners looked like gang members. There uniforms were a dark brownish green and they had black insignia in patches on shoulders and chests that resembled tattoos. Most of them were steroid buff and some looked like ex military and some looked like criminals.

One of the Gooners leading the group said, "Sano I need you to face the other way and get on your knees in front of the table."

Sano must have been following instructions because the Gooner said, "Good. Now lower your head on the seat and put your hands behind your back."

Two of the Gooners entered the cell with chains and handcuffs.

The leader of the Goon Squad said, "Stay face down on your bunk up there Boxer. This will only take a minute."

We heard the chains being wrapped around Sano's legs and waist.

The lead Gooner: "Okay stand him up…Now back out of the cell Sano…Okay we're headed for the side door…Time for you to visit your friends in Solitary Sano."

We heard Boxer's cell door slam shut and a minute later the building was silent again.

Chapter 6

Yard For Asians Only

In the morning after breakfast was brought to our cells, the gun tower announced, "Yard release for the Asian inmates only!"

Boxer pounded on our wall and said, "You guys will get off lockdown quick. This prison needs you guys to help run the place with us and the Blacks locked down!"

A Black inmate nearby yelled, "That's right. We need you guys makin our food, cleanin our clothes and takin out our trash!"

That sentiment irritated me but I had compassion for the fact that both of their races had been stuck in slow motion lock down for six months. Being confined to a cell the size of a small bathroom for that long did something to a human's psyche. I had been through it several times and knew that one of the negative after effects was that being around people in a crowd was unbearable. There were other problems associated with being in Solitary, like loud noises that caused massive anxiety, or a hypersensitivity to light, fast movement, or to people being offensive.

In the afternoon the gun tower announced, "Mark Grisham! They want you in the Program Office."

His cell door popped open and a few minutes later he showed up at our cell with a cup of coffee in his hand and a big smile.

He whispered, "I forgot to tell you guys something. We have a new guy who is making a lot of noise in building Five."

I asked, "What prison did he come from?"

Mark whispered, "Calipatria. He is a really big Skinhead from Venice and goes by Hitler."

I asked, "What's his problem?"

Mark whispered, "He wants to know who has the yard for the White inmates because he isn't getting fed. He says we should be sending chow hall food to those who don't have any."

I didn't blame him for that. A closed mouth didn't get any yum yum's.

I said, "Tell him that is need to know info he'll get soon enough. Tell him to send his paperwork for us to look over."

Mark came back from the Program office six hours later with the paperwork. He whispered, "Hitler wants to know why you guys have the yard for the White inmates and still stabbed Godwin."

I couldn't believe what I was hearing. We were being questioned blatantly. I pulled in his paperwork and listened to Damon whisper yell, "Who told him we had the yard and stabbed Godwin?"

There was silence on the other side of the door. I leaned as far as possible to see Mark's face. He was keeping it hidden at the extreme side of the door. It was obvious he told him. It was possible that he didn't, but highly unlikely. It was time to find out if he would lie.

He didn't. He whispered, "I did. He came at me hard with so many assaultive questions that I blew it."

I couldn't help but laugh at his honesty.

He whispered, "Sorry homeboys. What do you want me to do?"

Damon whispered, "Stop talking so much about heavy business."

I studied Hitler's court and prison paperwork while Damon continued to train Mark with better etiquette.

Hitler started coming to prison at 18 years old for violence. He was a White Supremacy type. As he got older and kept coming back for prison sentences, his charges got less violent and were drug and petty theft related. I imagined him coming from a broken home and finding an identity on the streets.

His prison paperwork started at Corcoran on a very serious and deadly yard. After some time there, he went to Calipatria, another very serious and deadly prison, very similar to this one, very close by.

At Calipatria he was used as a soldier by whoever was in control of the yard for the White inmates. He was ordered to stab an inmate on the yard. On his Solitary Confinement paper work, a Lock Up Order form

144-D, it stated he did 9 months on his SHU Term.

Hitler had left notes on the paperwork to help other people he sent it to understand other details. In pencil it stated: Drug Debt Whacking.

I considered his highly aggressive style in two ways. He could be hyper sensitive like me and just be exerting himself enough so that he didn't get used again. Maybe he wanted enough control to use his experience to create drug debt policies to avoid a race war without having to stab someone for not being able to pay for a heroin habit, like me.

Or he was a "dying to be someone" type, who was a professional "instigator" and "attention whore".

I knew both types well since I had graduated from one to the other. I also knew how to find out where he was on his path upon meeting him in person, on the yard.

I whisper asked Mark, "Run the make down on him."

Mark questioned, "What do you mean?"

"What does he look like, tattoos, gang, attitude, maturity level, brains..."

Mark hesitated like he was in unfamiliar territory.

Damon whispered, "It's a little late to clam up homeboy. You told him we were the shot callers for the yard and that we stabbed Godwin."

I would have laughed out loud if our situation weren't always deadly.

Mark answered, "He's big, early 30's, shaved head, tattoos..."

Mark ran out of material.

I said, "So you just told us about 90% of the White inmates."

Damon got to the heart of the matter, "Does he look like he can beat either of us up?"

Mark stepped away from the crack at the side of our cell and looked at us carefully and shook his head no slowly. He came back to the side and whispered, "He isn't as hard as either of you. He's big but its baby fat compared to you guys."

I asked, "Are his eyebrows shaved?"

Serious Skinheads shaved their eyebrows during times of war. Not all, but most of the ones that always kept their eyebrows shaved, were trying to hard.

Damon asked, "What Skinhead click?"

Mark didn't say anything. He was a terrible inquisitor. Because of that, he was easy to manipulate and move around like a chess piece.

I helped him understand and asked, "What do his tattoos say?"

Mark whispered, "I don't know."

Damon stopped whispering and said, "Your fired homeboy."

I laughed loud enough to lighten the mood, but said, "You suck Mark."

Damon schooled him on the art of anti bullying. He whispered, "Anytime you are being drilled like that you have to go offensive."

I finished the degree in prison psychology and said, "You should have responded by hitting him with high powered questions like a jackhammer like this, "What gang do you claim? What neighborhood do you run around in? Who brought you in? Who do you check in with? Who can cosign who you are? What do you specialize in on the streets?"

Mark looked like he was in way over his head. He came back to the side of the cell and whispered, "Those are some intrusive questions."

Damon whispered, "He's questioning our ability to run the yard after just stabbing the first violator."

I didn't even bother whispering and asked from in front of the door, "You don't see a problem with that?"

Damon said, "We should be commended for running such a tight ship."

I followed up with, "And for knowing how to run down policies with the Mexicans to keep another riot from happening."

Damon asked, "Did you at least speak highly of us about those things?"

Mark didn't say anything and that spoke volumes. He stammered, "I see what you mean. I blew it. He came at me hard and fast."

I changed the subject, "When are we getting yard?"

Mark was on better footing and he said, "Probably tomorrow. Heart said, "We might even get dayroom tonight after chow."

Chapter 7

Dayroom

The White and Mexican inmates shared half the inside of the building considered the "dayroom". The Asian and Black inmates shared the other half. The showers were also marked territory on both sides, but in the middle of the building, behind the podium 20 feet there were another set of showers on both floors. I realized I knew one of the Asians putting his towel on the bottom shower rack. That meant our showers were upstairs in that area.

Standing next to me, Damon said, "I guess we shower on this side and up stairs in the middle."

I nodded my head and said, "That Asian goes by K-9."

K-9 was a Vietnamese Gangster who was in the Orange County Jail with me. At 5'2 and in his late 30's, he was doing a life sentence for murder. His body was a portrait of Asian tattoo ink from his neck down over a body full of bunched up muscle. He had been the leader for the Asians in the cell modules of Theo Lacy Jail.

Damon said, "He looks like a warrior."

I said, "He is."

I scrunched up to the crack in the cell door and yelled, "Excuse me on the tier! K-9! What up? It's BJ!"

K-9 looked in our direction and I waved my hands in front of the Plexiglas window. He squinted his eyes even further than normal and asked in a heavy Vietnamese accent, "Who dat? Who kno my name?"

I yelled out, "It's BJ from K Mod at Theo Lacy!"

K-9 walked the edge of the dayroom five feet away from the cells so he didn't step into the side of the dayroom that we shared with the Mexicans. He turned the corner and recognized me and smiled from ear to ear. He yelled out, "What up Bugs? When you get here?"

When I was with him in county jail he could never pronounce my name BJ so somehow we were good with him calling me Bugs.

I yelled out, "I just got here."

K-9 said, "You no Spanky is here! He my cellie!"

He pointed to the other side of the dayroom and I saw Spanky sitting at a four person table playing cards, probably Pinochle.

Spanky looked exactly like Spanky on the Little Rascals, but the Asian version. He was only 19 years old and was also doing a life sentence for murder. Even though he could pronounce my name, BJ, he called me Bugs also because K-9 did.

Spanky got up from his table and walked the edge of the dayroom from the other side.

He yelled, "Hey Bugs! You need anything?"

Back in the county jail we always asked each other if we needed anything. It was a common courtesy. I yelled out, "No thank you! I'm good."

Garcia was sitting at the podium watching us with an amused look on his face. K-9 saw me looking at him and walked back the way he came along the edge of the dayroom for 20 feet until he got to the middle and passed the stairs where he could go to get to Garcia. I heard him ask, "Can I go talk to Bugs?"

Garcia looked at me with a confused look on his face. He probably thought he was hearing my AKA.

K-9 got to our cell. He said, "I go back to court soon for a retrial."

I knew he had been in the county jail for six years fighting his case. He had an expensive, high-powered attorney. It usually didn't help in Orange County. In this case, maybe it had.

I said, "Good luck. Hope it works out for you."

He said, "The Appeal Court ruled evidence no good for trial so maybe I get out."

I had seen Orange County allow evidence back in through an entire new trial that had been ruled out. It was a last gasp effort to try to keep the inmate they had decided was guilty for at least another year and more money spent on court paperwork, filing motions and hearings.

The guard in the tower tapped on the microphone to signify an announcement. "Attention in the building! Dayroom for the White inmates! You're off lockdown already!"

Chapter 8

Sometimes, I Don't Love This Life

Our cell door popped open. We gathered our shower gear and wrapped our towels around our necks. I already had my eye on the table and the exact seat I wanted.

I stopped at Boxer's cell and he was standing there watching. He was a few inches shorter than me at just less than six feet tall. In a place where almost all the inmates shaved their heads, he had black hair combed back. Unlike most prisoners, he didn't have a collage of tattoo patterns down his body either. His eyes were inky pools of brown seriousness, but there was laughter and compassion in there also.

He nodded to both of us and went to the crack at the side of his cell for privacy and said, "Glad you guys got away with it."

I deflected the attention and said, "You miss Sano already eh?"

He smiled and said, "That was my road dog. He was the best cell brother I ever had. It was like I wasn't even doing time."

Damon and I nodded our head we understood.

The guard in the gun tower wanted us to close our cell door and showed us by pushing the button that opened our cell. It made a "Clack…Clack…Clack" sound and the rollers kept grinding that sent it down the gutter.

I leaned in close to Boxer's cell and asked, "Can you hold our wine for us again?"

Boxer didn't hesitate and said, "Of course. Another mission already?"

Damon went back in our cell and grabbed the wine. It was in a pillowcase to camouflage it enough. He set it on the ground and pushed some of it under the cell door.

Boxer grabbed it and pulled it all in.

Damon closed the cell door and said, "I'm going to grab us a table down there. You need anything Boxer?"

Boxer said, "Not right now. Thank you."

I looked at Garcia. He was staring at us. I decided that I shouldn't take advantage of his good nature by staying at Boxer's cell. It would be good form if I did my workout, then got my shower, and then asked Heart if I could go talk to Boxer. I knocked on Boxer's door and said, "I'll be back in a little."

Mexican and Black inmates stood at every cell door watching. I avoided eye contact. There would be time to study who was in which cells later.

I passed 7 cells before the corner turned at a right angle where another row of cells extended for 17 more cells and passed stairs, the upper showers and another set of stairs before another corner.

I walked down the first set of stairs and Garcia was staring at me. He waved me to the podium.

I faced him for just long enough to be respectful and looked past him at the cells behind. Most of the time I had a sixth sense and zeroed in on which cells had the most energy. Not this time, it was to evenly spread out so far.

I looked back at Garcia just as he said, "So they call you Bugs. Is that like Bugs bunny or Bugsy Segal?"

I smiled. This was the first chance he was getting to run a make on me and it was going to look like I was lying, but I explained anyway. "I go by BJ not Bugs, but he couldn't pronounce BJ while we were in the County Jail so we just rolled with what he could."

Garcia looked even more confused. He said, "But the other Asian inmate called you Bugs also."

I hated to look like a liar. I was about to say something I shouldn't, like, explain that K-9 was an Asian shot caller so Asians beneath him would call me Bugs out of respect for him. Instead, I called Spanky.

Spanky came to the podium and the entire building was watching us. I said, "Spanky would you tell Garcia that K-9 can't pronounce BJ so he calls me Bugs."

Spanky's chubby face lit up in a smile over the memory. He said, "He can't say BJ."

Garcia looked like he understood but asked anyway, "Why do you call him Bugs? You just said BJ just fine."

With a straight face, like it should be understood, Spanky said, "Because K-9 calls him Bugs."

I smiled at Garcia and said, "All in the name of respect."

While I was talking about respect and letting Garcia see how I rolled, I asked, "What is your program like for dayroom? Can I work out and do handstand pushups against the wall?"

Garcia nodded his head and said, "As long as it's only one or two of you. I don't want the entire dayroom working out together."

I nodded my head and said, "OK."

Garcia continued, "If you hear the vestibule door opening stop working out to see if it's a Sergeant or anyone higher. Don't front me off."

I nodded my head and asked, "After I finish my dayroom business and shower can I go upstairs and talk to my friend in cell 211?"

Garcia looked up at Boxer's cell. He knew he was the Mafia on the yard. He was probably wondering who I was and how I was connected to him. He nodded his head and said, "I'll give you five minutes."

There were 10 tables cemented to the ground on our side of the dayroom and they were all empty except for one. Damon was at the table I wanted next to the stairs underneath our cell. It had the best vantage point of our side of the dayroom and felt like it was positioned like a seat against the wall in a bar or restaurant that saw everything entering and all the other key things.

I sat down next to him. He was stressed out. His face was tight and his eyes were focused like laser beams. When Damon's blood pressure was up, he talked really fast but his lips didn't move. Without opening his mouth much, he let out a string of cuss words with a few others that ended with, "F'ing Mark needs to stay in his cell if he can't represent better."

I felt the stress of possibly being called out at yard by one of our own kind. Deep inside me I was already imagining a confrontation. If there was one, it would explode right there, on the spot. There wasn't any room for backing down, or walking away in prison.

Mark had set the tone that we didn't know what we were doing by allowing Hitler to run over him. By not defending us in a certain way that showed a high level of respect and secrecy, he had belittled us to the point that Hitler was probably assuming we weren't as qualified as him. He was riding high off his recent "Whacking" that put him in Solitary for 9 months.

Even though I was betting that it was more likely than not that we would be involved in a power struggle explosion over it, I wasn't as consumed at the moment as Damon because I was studying the building's atmosphere. I was confidant and said, "Let's work out to release this steam."

Damon followed me to the wall underneath and just to the right of the gun tower. There was 10 feet of wall space before a couple of payphones for collect calls.

I leaned down and put my hands an equal distance from each other about 6'inches away from the wall and threw my legs up in a handstand. I had a bunch of pent up energy mixed with adrenaline from living on the razor's edge in a high powered and deadly California prison. That combination equaled a set of 30 easy and powerful reps. I kicked my feet together and threw them off the wall and landed perfectly as if I had just finished a back handspring like a gymnast. My confidence increased that I could handle whatever came my way.

Damon said, "Show off."

I knew he felt better seeing how comfortable I was. I reinforced it by saying, "Come on stud, show me what you're working with."

Damon was taller than me with longer arms so his set wasn't quite as proficient. Never the less, he was strong and obviously capable.

He was still muttering anger over being questioned by another high-powered White inmate, "F'ing dude better be careful or he'll get his head peeled like an onion."

I made light of the situation with the voice of reason. "He's probably just another White brother doing the best he can."

We did 10 sets of handstand pushups and showered. I went up the stairs to Boxer's cell.

With my back to the wall, facing the gun tower guard and Garcia below at the podium, I watched Damon. He looked like he was calmer, standing in front of a cell and talking to a Mexican inmate at another cell door.

Boxer told me about the prison he was at in Colorado.

"We were 7 floors underground. I was housed with the biggest of the biggest Mexican Mafia, Aryan Brotherhood, all the most well known bombers and terrorists."

I asked, "Who had the most juice?"

I knew that the Mexican Mafia and Aryan Brotherhood had the most influence but was curious to see how it was exerted in Colorado.

Boxer said, "You know the answer to that but the system has us all pinned down. Just to get to our cell, there was another cell door entrance like a vault, so we couldn't see other cells or fish a line out to communicate."

This was new information so I asked, "What were the cells like? Bigger and better than these?"

Boxer said, "Way bigger, way better."

We ran out of material to talk about pretty fast so it fell into the dark and ugly pit of the high-powered name game.

Boxer started dropping breadcrumbs to see who I knew and who I was connected to. He said, "They had a lot of Texas Aryan Brotherhood where I was at. Do you know Big…"

I said, "Nope. I don't know any of those dudes from Texas other than what I saw on TV about them all loosing their minds from doing meth. It looked like they all started telling on each other."

Boxer mentioned some more Mexican and White Mobsters who were housed with him in Colorado. Through our conversation I could see he was betting that I was affiliated with either the Aryan Brotherhood or the Nazi Low Riders, known as the NLR.

I told him, "I'm not validated as a gang member and don't claim nothin."

Boxer said, "Me neither."

I didn't know if he was just sticking to his story and stayed under the radar, or if he really wasn't an integral component to the largest underground gang in the world.

Then I realized he was just like me, a drug addict who happened to be an influential one. He said, "I just did drug business with some large people. Half of my family deals drugs and the other half work for Law Enforcement."

I explained some of my research into the drug war and where the Criminal Justice system interrupted me. Like reading page after page in a book, we were learning about each other and even more trust was being gained.

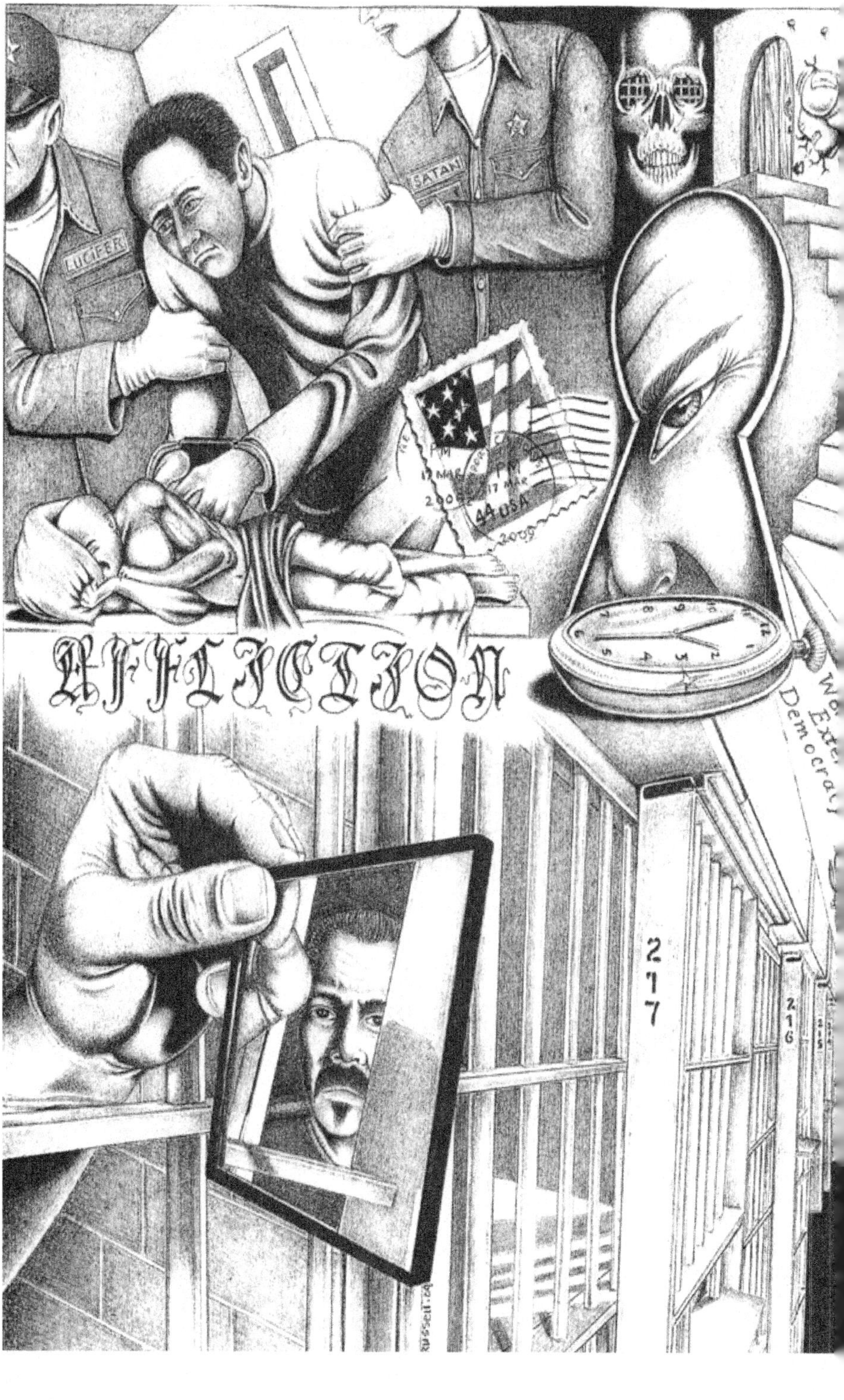
LUCIFER
SATAN
44 USA
AFFLICTION
217
216

Chapter 9

My Turn to Stress

Damon was lying down flat on his back on the top bunk. At over 6'3, his long, angular body extended further than the sheet metal his mattress sat on. His size 12 feet rested over the edge with both his heels touching while he waved his feet back and forth. It was one of his idiosyncrasies. It meant that he was comfortable. That irritated me.

Now I was the one stressed out. I couldn't sit or lie down. My mind was going to fast.

Our tier was going to get yard soon and there was a good chance Hitler was going to question us.

I paced the cell waiting for Damon to stop waving his feet. It didn't stop. Like a clock, every second his feet clacked together and continued to wave.

I stopped pacing. I sat down and grabbed a razor we kept to sharpen pencils and looked at it. I picked up another state issue single blade razor and took it apart.

I heard Damon's feet stop clacking. I felt him lean over to see what I was doing.

Without looking up at him I said, "It's about time you stop waving your feet back and forth like nothings wrong."

Damon asked, "What are you makin homeboy?"

He knew.

I emptied an ink pen of the cartridge inside, cut it with the razor so it was only 4'inches long and positioned the blade into the open end. I had to bite down on the end of the pen to flatten it enough to slide the blade in further. The edge of the blade peeled a plastic line away from the inside of the cylinder as it fit snugly deeper and deeper until just an inch of blade was extending out the end of the pen. I put the cap back on over the razor's edge. It was a tiny and deadly carving tool.

I said, "I'm just getting ready for yard."

I knew it wasn't cool to slice someone over a power struggle misunderstanding. In California prisons those kinds of wars were fought with ice picks or bone crushers. Razors were reserved for "Child Molesters".

But our ice pick was gone. We had one buried on the yard, but it didn't have a handle.

Damon asked, "Is that for Hitler if he gets crazy?"

I got up and nodded my head and said, "I'm sick of fighting. I want to make sure I win big."

Damon didn't like it. His face looked like he had a bitter taste in his mouth. He said, "I thought you said that he was just another White brother like us."

I paced the cell and calmed down. I said, "Yeah I know it's probably like that."

Damon helped me feel better by saying, "And you know I've got your back. You don't need that cutter tool."

I put it in my back pocket anyway and said, "You're right."

The guard in the tower tapped the microphone. He announced, "Attention in the building! Yard release for the White and Asian inmates on the top tier! Get ready for yard!"

Our cell door "popped" open. I felt adrenaline surging through my veins. I could feel it in my temples, squeezing in on me. Moving forward helped me think.

Out of my cell, I stepped to the side of Boxer's cell and didn't say anything. It was becoming a habit to check on him.

He asked, "Can you bring something to yard for me to send in to one of my homeboy's in 5 Building?"

I shook my head and said, "Not this time. Tomorrow."

I walked the tier and caught up with Damon at the stairs. The adrenaline was coursing through my entire body and I felt invincible, as long as I kept moving.

We passed the podium and the vestibule door clanked and grinded open for 5 seconds. It slammed home and locked giving us 6 feet of width to walk through. The tunnel was 30 feet long and I looked up through a thick bulletproof window that ran along a section of the roof to see the guard holding a block gun watching us. He walked above us to the opening above the vestibule tunnel.

We entered the yard underneath his gun hanging out the window. A tan concrete path led the way for 20 more feet to the asphalt track that circled the entire quarter mile yard.

Even though it was late afternoon, the 110-degree desert heat was suffocating. It immediately bit into my adrenaline surging energy.

I fought back against it by studying the yard for other White inmates. More than 150 yards away, on the other end of the yard in front of 5 Building, Hitler walked out of the vestibule.

He carried himself like a decorated soldier with the body language of a confident man. At well over 6 feet tall, his big baldhead was tilted back like he was always surveying things with a cynical outlook. He walked slowly, but precisely with his back arched as far upright as possible. I felt his demand for respect from across the yard and instantly disliked him more.

Instead of heading toward the confrontation, I was planning on him coming to us.

Damon asked, "How do you want to do this?"

I said, "I want to meet him by the pissers."

It was the best vantage point on the yard.

We walked the track to the first turn where the outside toilets and drinking fountain were just inside the curb into the yard. I stepped up on the curb and looked at the gun tower guard.

He was 60 feet away, down the line of asphalt track, sitting 30 feet in the air watching the yard. We were at the edge of his peripheral vision. He was staring at the inmates coming out of 3 and 4 Buildings directly across from him.

We had buried a shank the Mexicans left in our cell next to the sprinkler about 30 feet into the yard in the grass.

Damon saw me looking over there and said, "It doesn't look like you plan on talking."

I didn't want the buried shank. It didn't have a handle around the end of it. The ice pick shank I used to whack Godwin in the back of the neck had been a waste without the handle to hold on with. The first "hit" penetrated his neck, but hardly. The thin steel slid into my cupped hand right away, almost like a magic trick. Each additional "hit" from my right hand slamming into his neck was just my cupped hand, even though it looked like I was stabbing him. It was more for show.

Now, there might be heavy action.

Hitler was standing at our concrete table in front of 5 Building. He sat on top of the middle of it just like I would have, with his feet resting where you sit.

Gary, Horse and Rocky were in line shaking his hand.

Gary was an older White convict from San Bernardino who had the most influence for that area. Horse was from that neck of the woods also and knew of me from my business with the Hells Angels and Mexican Mobsters from the area 10 years ago. Rocky, also from that area, was a pit bull of a man who looked rabid and a little crazy. He was just over 6 feet and stacked with stocky, compressed muscles from over 20 years of prison workouts, weighing over 250 pounds. He was facing off with Hitler the same way he had with me a couple days ago. I laughed at the memory.

Damon laughed with me and said, "Rocky is a trip huh? That gap in between his front teeth and those crazy eyes should slow down Hitler's roll."

I calmed down a little knowing that Gary, Horse and Rocky had my back also. None of them would appreciate an instigator.

Rocky looked like he was done talking to Hitler and he, Gary and Horse walked toward us.

I studied Hitler's body language. He was an isolator. In his own way, he didn't bend to anyone else, and I respected that, but didn't respect that he was a divider.

Gary shook my hand and looked into my eyes. He said, "It looks like you're breathing fire and I know why."

Rocky smiled at how pissed I obviously was. He said, "We got ourselves an instigator over there."

Horse was almost a half a foot shorter than Gary and Rocky, but he was the oldest and knew me the best. He said, "I straightened him out that the yard was in good hands BJ."

Rocky grunted and said, "I told him he better be careful with his words."

Gary asked, "What are you going to do?"

I took the razor shank out of my back pocket and squatted down on the curb. I felt my angry energy bubbling into the point of rage and knew I didn't need the razor. I used my left hand to dig out enough dirt from the edge of the curb and buried the small weapon.

After a minute I said, "I want to talk to him over here. Will one of you go get him?"

Rocky said, "We'll go get him."

Gary, the veteran that he was, pointed something out and said, "Let's walk the track the opposite way so the tower guard doesn't watch us walk beneath him."

Gary, Horse and Rocky walked the track away from the tower guard toward the building we'd just come out of. From there, the track passed Building 2, then 3, then 4 where it turned and met the table Hitler was on in front of Building 5.

Hitler arched his body even more so he was looking as far down as possible at the group in front of him. He was getting off on the attention. He wasn't moving.

Rocky gestured with his head that I wanted to talk to him. Gary and Horse were nodding their heads also.

Hitler turned his neck our way a fraction and didn't move. Damon said, "He might not come to you."

I said, "The Art of War."

If I had to walk to him, there was very little chance I would hold my emotions in and make it back to the cell.

After another minute of frozen staring, Hitler got off the table. Rocky was the first to seize the opportunity and positioned his body as if he was an escort. Gary fell into a position on the other side of Hitler.

The group reached us and Hitler immediately distanced himself from Gary, Horse and Rocky in a way that showed disdain for them. Rocky caught the insinuation and grunted.

Damon caught it even further and was the first one to take the initiative. He treated Hitler with Skinhead lingo and said, "What's up comrad? I'm Rott from P@#'s."

Hitler smiled like he had finally found someone who didn't smell bad. He walked forward a few steps and hugged Damon.

I saw all of his hardened exterior melt away in an instant, exposing his maturity level. He was still a youngster, trying really hard, doing the best he could. Hitler was in his late 20's and looked like an albino. His skin was extremely white and clear. His blue eyes were magnified because of the contrast.

He was comfortable speaking in Skinhead lingo. He said, "What's up Skin? Good to finally meet a good comrad around here."

I didn't like the insinuation, that the rest of us weren't good. I said, "I checked your paperwork and saw the service you did at Calipatria."

Hitler's face lit up with a smile and it again showed me his maturity level. He was a big kid, but he was careful not to say much.

I continued, "Everyone of us has put in that kind of work."

Gary said, "Since you were in grade school."

I got to the heart of the matter and asked, "Did you say I couldn't whack someone because I have the yard?"

Hitler's face took on a serious look and he puffed himself up and said, "You aren't supposed to. A Shot caller calls shots and leads from the back."

I said, "Hitler pay close attention to this. I lead from the front and make sure everyone makes it through. If I want someone else to do something, I have to be willing to do it."

Damon said, "Hey comrad where did you get the wrong idea that the Shot caller can't handle business?"

We listened to Hitler. His communication skills were good, but the way he conveyed things wasn't.

He was under the impression that because at Corcoran, on the particular yard he was on, and at Calipatria, on the particular yard he was on, the Shot caller never put in work. He explained that it was done that way to insulate and protect the man in charge, so he could continue to benefit the entire race of inmates.

What he didn't understand was that was just a big con game.

Damon helped him understand and said, "BJ knows what he's doin brother."

Hitler stared at me with barely veiled contempt. I didn't look or act the way he expected a Shot caller should.

Part of me was hoping he'd challenge me. I said, "I don't respect Shot callers who force kids to put in work they aren't meant to put in. I was beaten as a kid, so I like to poke inmates who abused kids or beat up women. It works for my sense of justice. Do you have a problem with that?"

Hitler toned it down a little and shook his head no. He said, "I see what you mean but the Shot caller isn't supposed to risk himself and be the torpedo."

I understood what he was saying but helped him further. "If I didn't plan on getting away with it I would agree with you."

Everyone laughed remembering how I set up the job on Godwin.

I said, "There's another job to do. It's a hot one. Do you want to do it?"

Hitler's face changed. He knew he had dug his own hole. He stammered, "I just put in work and sat in Solitary for a year. Plus I have two strikes and don't want to catch a third strike."

Rocky grunted and said, "You should have thought of that before coming to prison."

The pressure was on Hitler to man up and say he would do it. He was looking weak.

He asked, "What kind of work is it?"

I answered a fraction, "I said it was a hot job. You know that means it's a stabbing."

Hitler tried to save face and said, "I know what it means. But what did the guy do wrong?"

Mafia business and Shot caller business wasn't done like that. The business end of things wasn't put on the table until after it was handled. I said, "The paperwork gets dropped after the hit, not before."

Hitler nodded his head and I saw a newfound respect in his body language. We were going to get along fine. He was just another White brother doing the best he could.

He said, "I'll do it if nobody else will."

I nodded my head and said, "Thanks, but not necessary. It's bottom tier business and we don't have time to wait for a bed move."

A friend of ours who answered to the name "Traveler" walked up to us. He half hugged Damon and then me and said "Thanks for the service you did for the yard the other day. I bet that dude won't ever beat another women in front of his 5 year old daughter."

I nodded my head that it was nothing. It really wasn't.

I noticed Mark Grisham come out of the program office and walk our way.

Traveler was still in 5 Building where Hitler was and I watched their interaction. Traveler was a Skinhead as well but he had problems with some high-powered ones in the past. It was nothing serious other than a power struggle and misunderstanding. In the Orange County jail, two of them jumped him, and got their Asses kicked all over the tier. Traveler was a good man who didn't use drugs in prison, or condone dope feign behavior.

He didn't seem to like Hitler that much. He didn't even look at him and I realized something. Hitler had probably tried to get Traveler involved in instigating with him.

I asked, "Traveler are you hungry over there?"

Traveler said, "I'm alright. I have some soups. Mark is starting to send in some chow hall food to us also."

Mark got to us and I pulled him aside to talk to Damon and I.

Relieved that the Hitler problem was solved, I faced the other one. I asked, "Did you find out what ANNLY/MOLEST stands for?"

Mark nodded his head and said, "It stands for Molesting and Annoying. Heart said there was only one kid being molested for years, but that there were prior offenses. That's why he caught a life sentence."

I already knew how we were going to handle it and started running down the first part of the operation. "I need you to get us out of the cell tomorrow morning for the bottom tier yard. Tell Heart we need to get some clothes from laundry or something."

Mark said, "He isn't stupid. He's going to know it's for something else."

I said, "Start with that to see if it works. If it doesn't, tell him we have to find someone to clean up that mess he gave us. I just don't want him thinking we are handling it yet."

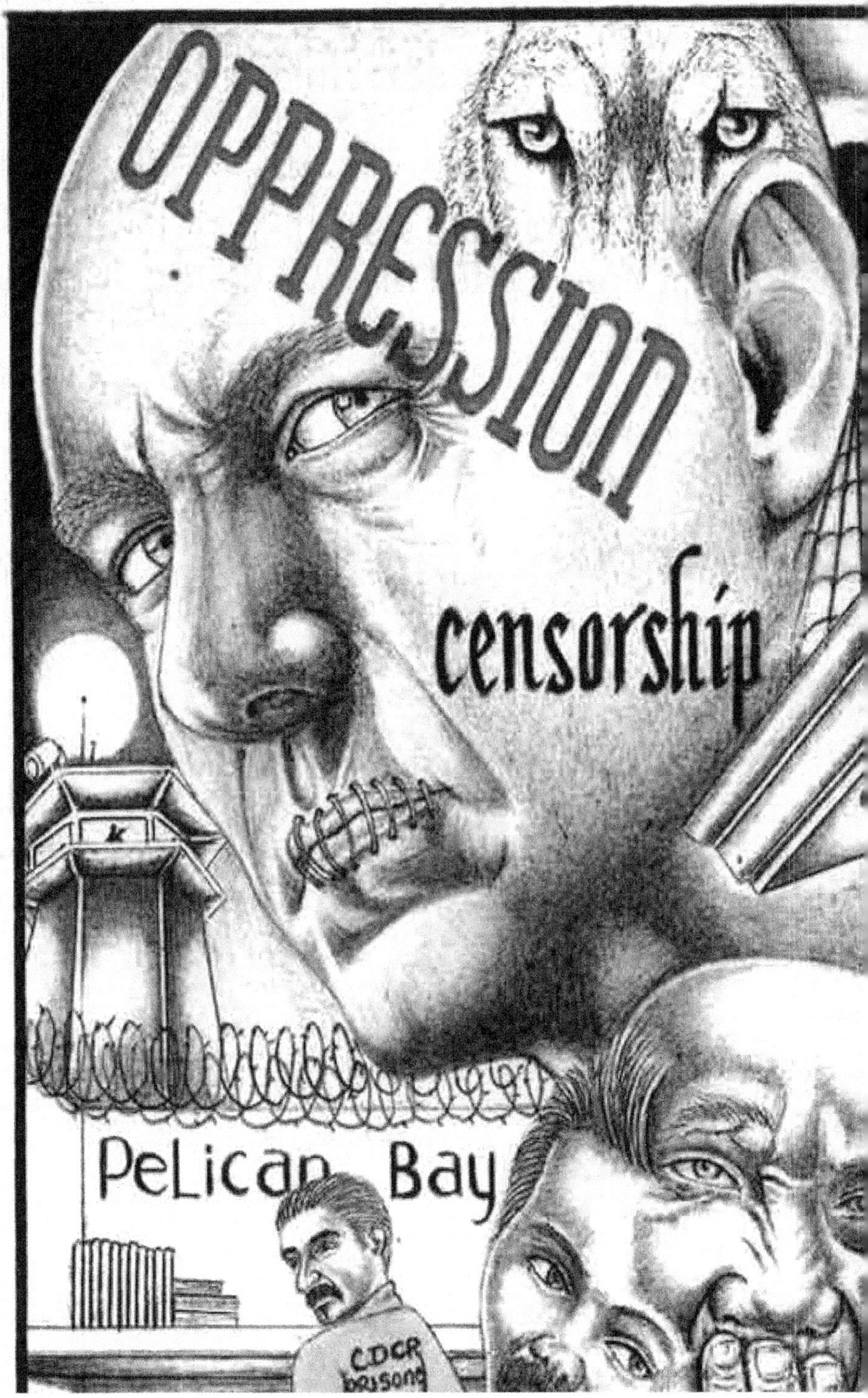
OPPRESSION
censorship
Pelican Bay
CDCR
prisons

Chapter 10

Down on the Yard

I pulled my line in from Boxer's cell. Attached inside a brown lunch bag were three state razors. In the message to him asking for them, I let him know what we had to do, by saying the yard was "going down" for a hot one.

I rolled up my mattress to expose the sheet metal bunk for Damon and I to sit on to construct our weapons.

We emptied two Bic pens and cut them down so they were four inches long with hollowed out cylinders.

I said, "Stick two razors in your pen facing the same way."

My razors were sticking out the open end a half-inch and the cap for the pen fit over it and closed, as if there wasn't something underneath.

I watched Damon finish constructing his tool and remembered something. When I pulled off the cap it would be nearly impossible to know which side the blades were facing, especially in the heat of the moment.

I said, "Make sure you know which side is the cutting end."

I used another pen to put a red dot on the outside of the cylinder facing the blade's edges.

I put the cap back on and with the weapon concealed, I asked, "Should we stick these tools in our Asses to take to yard?"

Damon saw me bend over and stick my hand behind my ass with the cut down pen inches from my pants.

I was joking but Damon wasn't sure. He caught on and said, "Only if you think we'll get searched going to yard."

Now that he mentioned it I realized it was possible. I stood at the cell door and watched what it felt like.

The guard in the tower tapped on the microphone to alert the inmates to an announcement. "Attention in the building! Bottom tier! Yard for the White and Asian inmates! Stand by!"

Cells started "popping" open down the tier below us. White and Asian inmates walked out of cells two at a time. The cells "popped" closer and closer to our cell until the last one opened beneath us.

Garcia looked normal standing at the podium. He was watching inmates meet and greet in the middle of the building where they marched into the vestibule tunnel.

It didn't look like anything unusual. But our cell never opened. The vestibule door shrieked and closed behind the last inmate and the building got quiet.

Damon said what I was wondering. "Mark couldn't get Heart to open us up."

I said, "It's coming."

There was a possibility that Heart wasn't working. Or, he wasn't going to give us the ability to maneuver him around, like he was with us.

Five minutes later our cell "popped" open.

With adrenaline surging through my veins the door slid on rollers right in front of me. I pulled it the rest of the way open and stepped out.

Boxer was standing at his cell door as usual. A weird thought took me captive. What if Daniel Dennings didn't come to yard for some reason?

I put my back to the wall next to Boxer's cell and whispered some of my fears. "We have someone who molested a child 44 times. If he comes out this morning we're getting him."

Boxer said, "Make sure you get away with it."

I tapped on his door with my knuckles in response and walked down the tier.

We exited the vestibule tunnel into the 110-degree desert heat. The sunlight was blinding.

We were wearing non descript state clothes that were blue denim with beanies covering our heads. Most of the inmates already on the yard were in grey shorts and a white tank top or no shirt.

We walked the asphalt track around the turn and stopped at the next corner by the pissers.

The guard in the gun tower 60 feet away, 30 feet in the air, was watching the yard directly in front of him. He wasn't paying attention to us in his extreme corner.

Directly underneath him, there were exercise bars that consisted of 8 pull up bars in a row that ended in another 3 pull up bars facing the other way at a right angle. Inside further, there were dip bars that accompanied the pull up bars. In further, there were flat steel benches to do sit ups or other exercises on.

The first 4 bars in the row, the furthest from us in the corner, were the ones that the White and Mexican inmates shared. Without the

Mexicans, there were only a dozen White inmates exercising.

Further into the yard, directly in the tower guard's view, about 50 yards away were the handball courts.

There was one wall 30 feet high. On one side the Asians played and on the other side the Whites played. The curb along the track had inmates standing up and watching or keeping score.

Building 3, where Daniel Dennings lived, was behind it. I scanned the rest of the yard looking for an inmate that fit Mark's description.

On the bottom tier there were 97 White inmates and 114 Asian inmates. It was impossible to find the child molester in the sea of inmates.

Standing on the curb next to me, Damon asked, "How are we going to do this?"

I said, "We're waiting for Mark to identify him. Then we're going to wait here and hope he comes to take a piss before yard recall."

The pissers were 20 feet away from us just inside the asphalt track where it turned the corner. I said, "When he walks there to take a piss or get a drink out of the fountain, we get him."

Damon nodded his head.

I explained further, "I want you to circle behind him on his way here. But you wait on me. Look into my eyes because I'm going to be facing you and the gun tower. When I look at you I'm either going to nod yes, or shake my head no based on where the guard is looking."

Damon nodded his head.

I continued, "From your vantage point you look behind me all the way to Building one to make sure nothing is wrong that way."

Mark Grisham came out of the Program Office almost 100 yards down the track. He walked the asphalt and stepped on the curb to survey the yard. He was getting used to us being posted up on the far corner and turned his head and saw us.

We watched him walk 100 yards down the length of the asphalt track. Heat waves simmered from ink black concrete that cooked at 140 degrees.

Mark stopped in front of us and said, "He should be coming out any minute. He works as a janitor who cleans the showers and comes out after he's done for an hour and a half."

I nodded my head and felt a lump in my throat pressing in on me I'd never felt before.

Mark continued, "I'm going to go over there and point him out as he comes out."

From 200 yards away we heard the vestibule door to Building 3 open right when Mark got close. A tall, older White inmate walked out of the tunnel by himself. Mark turned and looked our way and nodded his head.

Daniel Dennings walked the asphalt track toward Building 4 and followed the turn toward Building 5.

Mark followed him from 10 feet away until he stopped walking the track and stepped into the yard to talk to a couple of inmates playing chess on the bleachers.

Damon said, "Come on Mark, don't be so obvious."

The inmates sitting on the bleachers must have been in Building 3 with Daniel Dennings.

Mark looked uncomfortable and finally started walking the asphalt track again. He passed inmates working out. Some were doing pushups on the curb. Others were doing calisthenics in groups of two. Other inmates walked the track in groups of two or three. A few inmates jogged.

Mark walked up to us and asked, "Do you know who he is?"

Damon said, "Yeah homeboy that was pretty obvious."

Daniel Dennings stood watching the game of chess for an hour. It seemed less and less likely the vigilante yard justice was going to happen.

During that period, my mind was a turbulent consumption of conscience. Thoughts waged a war of good versus evil. It had to be right to cut this child predators face for all the kids he had ruined. Images of little innocent faces flashed through my mind's eye. Then, I imagined their damaged soul's tormented in inner afflictions that the devil seized on. Childhoods in ruin, sexual relations destroyed, and future families destroyed, all because of Daniel Dennings. I remembered some of my own childhood that sent me into a rage that found solace in the drug war as an active participant. Even though I saw Daniel Denning's evil and the after math, I saw that I had no right to be his judge and the hand of violent justice. Who was I to decide if he had repented?

My pride was right there to torment me. I couldn't walk away from this job, not in a prison where violence was the only solution.

With 10 minutes left before yard was over for the morning, Daniel Dennings walked away from the chess game at the bleachers, and got back on the asphalt track and walked to us.

He was headed to the pissers.

Damon circled him and I looked at the guard in the tower. He was holding a block gun in his hand and staring the other way. I looked back at Damon right as he looked into my eyes. I gave a slight nod and pulled the cap off the pen to find the red dot.

Daniel Dennings was 6 feet from me and I let my adrenaline go and rushed him. He gasped first and responded by throwing his hands up in the air a split second after the blades connected just below his right ear and slashed downward to his chin.

Damon caught him in the next instant with a slice to the other side of his neck.

I turned at a sharp angle and marched in a hyper walk away from the pissers into the grass at an angle across the yard taking me to the handball court.

I almost threw my pen shank of razors but held on as a thought struck me that there might be finger print evidence. To make that less likely, I pulled on the razors and felt a pile of skin that had built up, slide like goo with the razors as they came out of the pen cylinder. I dropped one razor and marched onward another 15 yards and dropped the other razor.

After I got half the distance to the handball courts from the scene I looked back. I looked for Damon and didn't see him. I found Daniel

Dennings staggering on the asphalt track under the tower waving his arms everywhere. The tower guard noticed and so did the inmates near the work out bars who scattered away from him.

A second later the alarm sounded. It screeched a high pitch whine that rose and fell in decibels.

The gun tower yelled into a microphone that sent his voice through speakers, "EVERYONE GET DOWN!! DOWN ON THE GROUND FLAT ON YOUR STOMACHS! GET DOWN!"

I walked even faster with only a few seconds left before I would stand out as the last man standing. I got to the handball court wall and circled behind it in the only blind spot on the yard from the gun tower.

As I got down and sat Indian style for a second, I peeled off the blue denim jacket that had been buttoned to the chin. Underneath, I had on a white tank top like everyone else. I used the blue denim jacket like a blanket and got down on my stomach, in the prone position, like everyone else.

The sounds of each building's vestibule doors shrieking open were followed by guards running into the yard to look for action to quell.

Mark stood in front of the Program Office and watched the door open. A Lieutenant walked out, followed by a Sergeant, followed by Heart.

Medics ran a stretcher to a now lying down Daniel Dennings.

Where was Damon?

The entrance to D Yard's gate opened next and an army of I.G.I. guards stormed the yard in a fast walk.

They circled Daniel Dennings and looked where he pointed, toward the pissers.

For the next hour every inmate stayed on the ground watching. Guards allowed inmates to move off the 140-degree asphalt to get back on the ground flat on the dirt and grass while the I.G.I. set up the crime scene tape and took pictures.

To be continued…

Dear reader,

It is with sincere gratitude that I would like to thank you for reading **The Art of War: A Prison Memoir.** I truly hope this book has been an eye opening experience. If you have enjoyed this book, ***please consider being kind enough to leave a review on Amazon.*** It would be helpful to other readers and me. Tap this link and scroll down about halfway on the left to where it says,

want to leave a review~ http://amzn.to/14x5nMT If you can share it on Facebook, Twitter or anywhere else I thank you! If you want one of my other books and can't afford it, I will gift one. You can contact me at rollcallthebook@gmail.com or friend me on Facebook to keep up with updates and praise reports here~ https://www.facebook.com/glennlangohrcalifornia
Would you rather listen to my books? Here is a complete list of my audio books~ http://amzn.to/1aeliPs

Writing this book was a purging of my soul. I am not proud of any of the things I did, but it was the best I could do at the time. Now, with many years of freedom from prison, I am actively seeking to help others recover from drug and alcohol addiction, and other afflictions those addictions mask. God Bless You.

        You can contact Glenn:

Author Page:
http://www.amazon.com/-/e/B00571NY5A
Author Page UK:
http://www.amazon.co.uk/-/e/B00571NY5A
Blog:
http://rollcallthebook.blogspot.com/
Smashwords:
http://www.smashwords.com/profile/view/lockdownpublishing.com
Facebook Pages:
https://www.facebook.com/glennlangohrcalifornia
https://www.facebook.com/lockdownpublishingdotcom
https://www.facebook.com/KindlePrisonStories
Twitter:
https://twitter.com/#!/rollcallthebook

Other Books by Glenn Langohr~

MY HARDEST STEP TO STAY SOBER

GLENN LANGOHR

ROLL CALL
Prison Sto...

GLENN LANGOHR

PRISON STORIES
THE COMPLETE COLLECTION
GLENN LANGOHR

UNDERDOG
PRISON RIOT
RACE RIOTS
LOCK UP DIARIES: DRUG DEBTS
GLADIATOR

A RAW DESCENT INTO CALIFORNIA PENAL HELL

CAUGHT IN THE CROSSFIRE
LIFE IN LOCKDOWN

GLENN LANGOHR